Travels with Tessy

Tessy Braun

CONTENTS

Photographs

ACKNOWLEDGMENTS

In addition to my parents I would like to thank my poetic friend Billy Harrington for supporting and encouraging my poetry, and the publication of this book. You have helped me tremendously Billy, and you have been a wonderful friend, so thank you from the bottom of my heart.

Furthermore I would like to thank the Instagram poetry community for all the love and support you have given me. In particular Sarah Oltean, Rob Dale, Shelley Cooper, Kat Cheesewright, Jeffery Egenlauf and Emma Batchelor, Melanie Haagman among many more.

Love from Tessy x

The Magic of Cornwall

Nowhere in this world touches me so,
as does my favourite place to go.
To the South West of England -
where Cornwall is my true adoration,
steeped in mystical sensation.

Oozing such magical ambience,
ancient stones, King Arthur and castles,
piskies and changelings, giants and other rascals,
like Mermaids, Bucca and Spriggan.

Full of curiosity, and often with ferocity,
as fishermen know all too well.

In my opinion nowhere can compare
to Cornwall's awe-inspiring atmosphere.
Shipwrecks and ragged coastlines,
secret beaches and mysterious old mines,
with their engine houses scattered on the cliffs.

Tessy Braun

St Ives Bay

St Ives Bay,
endless golden sand
lined with rolling dunes.
Hear the sea whisper the ocean tunes.
Look out beyond the breaking waves,
Godrevy stands tall all night and day.

But among the Upton Towans lie
a factory once of dynamite,
ruins of buildings still standing by
make great adventures for you and I.

Memories of this holiday park
are sweetly mixed up into one.
This is where we used to come
when my sister and I were only young,
and throughout the years we would return.
Now it is my children's turn...

To climb in the park overlooking the bay,
to go to the arcade in the evening to play.
To make sand sculptures and build lots of castles,
to splash in the water enjoying a paddle.
To eat chips in the conservatory café,
and to play ball and games till the sun goes away.

A Window to Paradise

A window straight to paradise,
from inside our cosy caravan,
we love to stay at St Ives Bay,
so visit whenever we can.

Even though it's autumn,
and October chills our bones,
the sea view is enticing,
Just like a second home.

We climb the rolling sand dunes,
explore each hill and mound,
absorbing delights of the scenery,
and the roaring ocean sound.

Then to stroll the golden stretch,
a beach four miles long,
there is no other place to which
I could say my heart belongs.

St Ives, Cornwall

Perched up on the edge of St Ives town,
from the car park on the hill so high,
see the harbour – look right down,
lichen covered roof-tops below you lie.

Strolling through the narrow streets,
browsing the quaint little shops,
buy some fudge or other treats,
some saffron bun or St Ives rock.

A walk over the island is nice,
watch out for rare species of birds,
Black Tern, Guillemot and Sabine's Gull
have all been sighted (so I have heard).

Sit on wooden beams by the beach,
children climb ropes that moor the boats,
sunken in sand without water they lie,
until buoyant again with the incoming tide.

Eat fish and chips from the Balancing Eel,
(be careful, for those nifty crooks may steal!).
Then after this delicious tea time meal,
we trek back up that steep old hill.

Lelant to St Ives

The prettiest tracks I have ever known,
parallel to a stretch of coast.
Outstanding beauty before your eyes,
the railway from Lelant to St Ives!

Look out across Porthkidney Sands,
observe Godrevy and where it stands,
you'll see a slightly different view,
that rocky island is split in two!

Once you've passed Carbis Bay,
ends the St Ives Bay railway,
a pleasant journey and not too far,
without all the stress of parking the car!

The Coastguard Helicopter

The ocean flat like a glistening sheet of glass,
apart from the soothing ripple of gentle waves,
and the occasional enormous breaker
that rises like a tsunami,
crashing in a cacophony of white water swash.

A colourful montage of bobbing boards,
rubbery black seal-like beings cling on.
Suddenly a noise and every one looks up,
squinting in the sun's early evening glare.
The Coastguard Helicopter is coming from the west!

Gasps from the beach as the paddlers
point at the unexpected spectacle
which advances towards the surfers.
Whirring and chopping furiously as it speeds overhead,
at such a very low height
that the crew are seen waving from inside.

Anticipation of the helicopter's arrival
gives way to pure excitement.
My son and I catch a wave to the shore,
and his little brother squeals with joy
at how near to the ground it flew.
An exhilarating highlight to our afternoon.

This time the display is a training exercise
and thankfully no emergency call out.
Yet often scrambling to a cliff rescue
or to the capsized out in the ocean,
these valiant and brave life savers
protect us from the perils of the sea.

Porthcurno

Drawn towards the turquoise bay,
we couldn't let the steep cliff get in our way,
it was such a Godly beautiful day,
the finest weather so far on our holiday.

The cliff path descent was manageable to a degree,
thinking of our reward (the azure Porthcurno sea!).
Yet after chasing the crashing waves,
it was time once again to be really brave.

The ascent - dizziness took hold,
all of a sudden I wasn't feeling so bold
(and kind of wished we had taken the road),
but instead of tuning into "survivor mode"
I started to whimper and my pace slowed.

I do wonder if I hadn't had my boys with me
would I have handled the climb more efficiently?
I crawled up on all fours in a tearful state
imagining how one mistaken step could seal our fate.

My older child had no fear,
for to the top of the cliff he was soon near.
As for my little one, he had no tears,
but was still wobbly and unpredictable in years.
What possessed me to attempt such a feat?
Believe me, it's a challenge I will *never* repeat!

Porthcurno II

How enchanting your colours are,
electric green and blue.
Hypnotising waves crawl up,
amazing what the moon can do!

Crashing down in mermaids' delight,
before gently lapping up the shore,
I could watch the waves all day till night,
This beach is a place I so adore!

The setting like no place on earth,
the sand gold and laden with shells,
ancient granite cliffs frame the cove,
the ocean waves they rise and swell.

I can't think of anywhere I'd rather be,
the place I love the most,
the magic of the Porthcurno Sea,
a mesmerising part of the Cornish coast!

Minack Theatre

You've never seen such a picture, I guarantee,
such as a theatre carved in the cliff overlooking the sea.
Natural cushions of grass from the seats now grow,
an open air playhouse for the "Atlantic-view" show!

This magnificent creation from a woman's dreams made
in nineteen thirty one thanks to Rowena Cade.
With help from her gardener and granite transported,
the efforts they made were certainly not thwarted!

For today we can visit over eighty years on,
take delight in storytelling, acting and songs.
The landscape picturesque as you may ever imagine,
so stand on the stage and set free all your passion!

Beach Days with Mum

I sometimes feel sad at the beach,
gazing at things that are just out of reach.
Thinking of memories of when we were little,
when our mum and dad were young,
and life had only just begun.

Then I look at my own two boys,
squealing and enjoying the sand and sea,
oh how the years roll on,
so many have been and gone.

One day my beach days will be full of sorrow,
when I think of what will happen in years ahead,
when the unspeakable is said.

Summer days with mum and my boys,
adventures and such intriguing talks.
Crabbing, Cornish pasties and rock pools,
sand sculptures, paddling and cliff walks.

Not always idyllic - life often isn't,
but these days will be reminiscent
in many years to come,
and long after the fun.

Seaside Chant

I'm on the beach and people-watching,
so many people here today,
there's families with children, couples too,
the young and the old, the happy and blue.

Canoes and body-boards bobbing around,
breakers making their 'crashing' sound,
chatter and laughter from left to right,
and children screeching in frenzied delight.

St Michael's Mount

We mosey over the sand at Marazion, the tide far out,
the causeway exposed with its uneven stones,
leading out to St Michaels Mount.

Waves abandon thick seaweed, strewn across the beach,
with wellies on we leap, squelch & screech,
the castle harbour we cannot wait to reach.

Our slog up the hill towards the island green began
to a storyteller, telling the tale of Cormoran,
(the giant who ate up animals from Penzance and all around).

Making the journey upwards to the house of St Aubyn, high
up at the top of St Michael's Mount in the sky,
spotting the giant's stone heart in the path as we pass it by.

Oh the views, the views! They're spectacular and stupendous,
through the castle windows the sea looks tremendous,
(though if you suffer from vertigo you'd find it horrendous!).

St Michael's Mount in Marazion, a day of Cornish myth,
a fantasy of history you can't afford to miss.
Special times here with my boys, I love to reminisce.

Standing Stones

Stonehenge is magnificent in all manner of ways,
yet the Cornish stones capture my imagination and amaze.

The stone circle of Boscawen-un
is a deeply eerie and mysterious one.
(At least it was when we paid a visit before,
with the fog low, we were alone on the moor).

Enigmatic are these ancient monuments,
we look upon them with astonishment,
soaking up the creepy atmosphere,
absorbing their energy by standing near.

The Mên an Tol with its curious hole
is an old friend of mine from when I was small.
On the road from Madron to Morvah,
we often call by to say hello, and then through we crawl.

Lanyon Quoit, Chûn Quoit and more,
Merry Maidens, Mên Scryfa,
Chysauster Ancient Village,
there's so much to explore!

Beware the sea

Never underestimate the sea,
for though I find it a comforting place to be,
its unrelenting power always astonishes me,
with deeply magic depths and alluring mystery!

Sea Doctor

No better remedy would I prescribe,
so to cleanse your spirit and your mind,
than to take a walk by the ocean-side.

Noise of waves crashing over rocks
helps confusion become unlocked,
clears a cloudy muddled brain,
and makes you feel alive again.

Tessy Braun

Land's End

Walk the rugged Land's End coast,
contemplate dramatic views.
ships once caught upon the rocks,
loss of life, the sea would choose
to swallow up a fateful vessel,
and let rot beneath the water level.

The wind will blow cool and strong,
the whispering ocean plays the song
of breakers whistling all night long,
a crashing dance; we sing along.
Looking out to sea forever,
stretching to "far-away" America.

End of land and most westerly place,
fierce and ferocious atmosphere.
Tourist attraction, come, make haste,
Walk the cliff away from here
to breathe the air and feel the earth,
to the place that is the last and first.

Winter Beach at Looe

Winter beach at Looe,
the sand all tossed about,
mounds of tangled seaweed
among shells and washed up driftwood too.

Beautiful to see,
despite the air so chilled,
the sea more strong and fierce,
the fresh air bites yet sets me free.

Clutching a small box,
collecting limpet shells,
freedom for us to run,
and nimbly clamber on the rocks.

Relubbus

Tucked up,
soft rain tapping,
so warm in hearts and body,
just the two of us,
(before there was the four of us),
by the sea in Relubbus.

A day spent,
waving at the bobbing seals,
a choppy ride to the Carracks,
ice creams too.
Body boarding in the blue,
the end of land in front of you.

Now relax,
a cuddle well deserved,
in a cosy caravan,
Chinese takeaway for tea,
we ate it up deliciously,
then you declared your love for me.

Widemouth Bay

The roaring, wild, choppy ocean
has a hypnotising motion,
waves rise up tall as walls,
up and up the water crawls.

Then crashing down in great commotion,
the sea displays her firm devotion,
fiercely kissing and caressing the sand,
graciously moulding the shape of land.

I was out there on my board,
clinging tight onto the cord,
those waves knock me to and fro,
then gliding to the shore I go.

Dreams of living by the sea

My dreams of living by the sea,
bring a certain comfort to me.
Yet to dwell two hundred miles from my family,
Also brings ambiguity,
over whether one day
I could make it a reality.

Black Head

(St Austell Bay)

Sticky and humid in the midday sun,
my rucksack strap is digging my shoulders
as we walk along the cliff path,
breathing in the fresh ocean air,
mixed with smells of the countryside.

Wild blackberries scattered in the hedges
make tasty snacks for hungry little tums.
the St Austell Bay; wide, vast and magnificent,
blue, like a giant sapphire,
under a cloudless sky.

Lansallos

Headstones centuries and centuries old,
cracked and weathered where rest those souls,
a creeping feel to the air around,
Lansallos village, away from the crowds.

Taking the road down from the churchyard,
a smugglers lane too narrow for cars,
the pebbly path that leads to the sea,
winding and long we trek precariously.

Stoney and slippery onwards we ramble,
Mother careful not to sprain her ankle,
for what would Mr Stitson say if he knew
she scrambled down on a knee so new!

A reward at the shore where we visualise
boats rowing in with smugglers inside,
and what horrors in the still of the night,
the smugglers faced in their treacherous plight.

Morwenstow

Curious, eerie Morwenstow,
where Mother wanted to show
where our ancestors lived a long time ago.

The atmosphere solemn and still,
where on approach tall hedges hide narrow lanes away,
and isolated ambience always remains the same.

We open the gate to the churchyard,
ancient headstones cling tightly onto the steep edges,
and rooks call out obscurely with their scratchy yelp in the early
evening sun.

Mysteriously the sea appears as though it may spill and submerge
the glebe completely,
such a perfect illusion while
just over the hills the cliff drops four hundred feet.

Oh, how we weep,
thinking of the many souls whose wrecks
came ashore on the rocks below.
In 1842 The Caledonia, one such ill-fated vessel,
carrying wheat to Falmouth was its true intention,
but, Parson Hawker in the night was faced with such horrors
beyond our comprehension.

Her figure head now hangs queerly in the church,
rescued once again from the temper
and gust of the Atlantic coast.

Hawker's Hut

Hawker's Hut, such a breath-taking scene,
dramatic, peaceful, quiet and serene,
made with driftwood, no doubt from wrecks
of old sea ships and their washed-up decks.

Parson Hawker would sit inside
snug in the cliff face while watching the tide,
writing his words and expressing his mind,
pipe in his hand - what a place to unwind!

It once was the whimsical vicar's retreat,
an impressive hideout with a round timber seat,
but now preserved for all of our pleasure,
Hawker's Hut, a real Cornish treasure!

Temple Church

Little church in Temple,
so easily not seen,
if not for my mother
I never would have been!

12th century sanctuary,
by Knights Templar's hand,
a safe refuge for pilgrims
travelling to the Holy Land!

Knights hospitalliers take over,
then over them, Henry the VIII,
pushed Temple into suppression,
no practice of Catholic faith.

Centuries on and re-created,
marry, no license or banns,
hasty lovers now elated,
famous across Cornwall's land!

In seventeen forty four,
little church in disrepair,
like Gretna Green no more,
end this unlawful affair!

The roof came tumbling down,
killed the vagrant where he slept,
now nothing more than a ruin,
but, Trevail dreamt of renewal yet.

Rebuilt; the Parish of Blisland,
high up on Bodmin Moor,
such a curious church
we now visit and adore.

Clean white-washed walls,
wooden chairs for pews,
stained glass so pretty,
from the graves, graceful views.

Little church in Temple,
so easily unfound,
just off the spine of Cornwall,
sacred history on this ground.

Jamaica Inn

Welcome to Jamaica Inn,
many curiosities lie within.
A roaring fire most inviting,
and history worth forever writing.

Sinister whispers in foreign tongue
once the dark night has begun,
footsteps walk the corridor,
Jamaica Inn on Bodmin moor!

Travellers who smuggle gin ashore,
stop by the inn at Bolventor,
to rest their souls till they awake,
then away to Devon they escape!

Roche Rock

Looming repelling giant,
a ghastly monstrosity!
Towering over the village,
with demonic ferocity.

Dominating countryside,
grey quartz and tourmaline,
the hermit once sleeping high up,
a Leper as legend writes him.

Craggy mossy boulders,
a muddied uneasy approach,
silhouettes in the chapel,
on route to imposing Roche.

Intrepid and curious,
the iron ladder perpendicular,
with shaky anticipation,
we climb this rock peculiar.

Progressing in altitude,
to greet this haunting abode,
a wary uncomfortable mood,
with devilry sure to unfold.

Bodmin Moor

Cornwall's bleak heather covered moor,
bronze age hut circles surrounding Rough Tor.
windswept and exposed, the moorland so lonely,
apart from the occasional Bodmin Moor pony.

Softer and smoother than neighbouring Dartmoor,
whispers in the wind circling the tors.
The echoes of the past trapped in vibration,
creating an eerie and haunting sensation.

Marshes and bogs into shallow valleys drain,
though a warm calm day would help to tame
the tempestuous wilderness of this Cornish heath.
Can you imagine the infamous Bodmin Moor Beast?

Bodmin Gaol - a location of horror and dread!
Listen out for the screams of the punished and dead
as you walk through the corridors where prisoners slept,
while the innocent convicts silently wept.

Does Excalibur still lurk in Dozmary Pool?
Legends and mysteries intriguing for all!
The lonely high moorland seems lost in time,
and a road slices through, known as Cornwall's spine.

Cornwall's bleak heather covered moor,
bronze age hut circles surrounding Rough Tor,
windswept and exposed the moorland so lonely,
apart from the occasional Bodmin Moor pony.

Murder on Bodmin Moor

High up on Bodmin moor,
I hear the whispers of the poor
soul that came too close to death,
and then to take her final breath.

Murdered by a jealous hand
on desolate and rugged land,
dead in the shadow of Rough Tor,
on the 14th April eighteen forty four.

A Cornish fable

The baby was soft, smooth and fair,
peacefully sleeping with a wisp of fine hair,
never a burden; a freshly new-born,
swaddled in blankets all cosy and warm.

On a stormy night, with the wind's howling scream,
dark all around but the silver moon beam,
with the window half open and curtain upswept,
the baby is gone, and something else has been left!

Peculiar whispers and gurgles unlike
the beautiful baby that was taken that night.
Its skin like a toad and its hair coarse and wild,
its cry like an animal, not of a child.

It wants to be loved and it wants a kind home,
old and craggy with a hideous groan.
But what of the baby, where did she go?
Only the goblins and pixies would know.

St Protus and Hyacinth, Blisland

Just north of Cornwall's spine,
sits Blisland, a beautiful find.
An extraordinary church and truly divine,
and one that has stood the test of time.

John Betjeman loved this church so,
the most beautiful church in the west to go.
He spoke of this gem on his radio show,
the only church pledged to the brothers in Rome.

A column supported by restoration,
vestry full of elaborate decoration.
Escaped its fate from Henry the VIII's
sixteenth century reformation.

NB Blisland Church was completely restored in the 19th Century. It looks today as it would have done before Henry VIII's depredation.

Kit Hill

We sat out that sunny afternoon in a giant fruit bowl,
two oranges basking in the sultry sun.

Surrounded by flawless views of the countryside,
from Brown Willy to Yelverton in our line of sight.

The hazy light blending the distant views,
but still beyond beautiful were those hues.

All the time a buzzing drone circling by - like a spy,
we wave, and talk of that strange robotic fly!

My mother can see the mine chimney on a clear day,
from her garden fifteen miles away!

Twenty years ago or more from Germany your sister came,
picked whortleberries a plenty, but we didn't see any today.

We sat out that sunny afternoon in a giant fruit bowl,
two oranges basking in the sultry sun.

My Childhood Home

To the comfort of my childhood home,
the nipping moor wrapped around us.
Yet inside the fire burning,
and tender memories returning.

Workings of the west Country line the walls,
trinkets scattered from our travels abroad.
On display, memoirs long since passed,
ensuring those moments will forever last.

Stretching on the feather bed I arise,
in pitch dark and hushed countryside.
Little arms wrapped around my waist,
from the floor pops up a second little face!

"Is it time to get up mummy?" they say,
eager to start the delights of their day.
Embedded in their hearts and minds,
visiting grandma is a very special time.

Sheepstor

Sun ferociously burning my back,
walking pole handy in case of some sort of attack.
Mother says don't walk the moor without a stick,
and wear long socks to protect from scratches and ticks.

Setting off on our expedition at Burrator,
my children have never climbed Sheepstor before,
and oh my! The view of that deep dazzling pool,
a reservoir glistening like a gigantic blue jewel!

So up and up we clamber across granite boulders,
enjoying the climb despite straps digging into my shoulders,
yet when we reach the very top - what an absolute treat,
with the wind relentless, but the whole world at our feet.

Haunting Formidable Dartmoor

Dartmoor bleak and wicked,
in a climate grey and cold,
on the edge of Dartmoor
my dear Mother is growing old.

Haunting formidable Dartmoor,
with her granite tors so steep,
howling wind, rain battering down,
of beasts and ghosts the locals speak.

Home to me was this barren land,
trees bent down by force of weather,
uninviting gorse and swaying fern,
skulls and bones among wild heather.

I often wish my mother was close,
and lived in the city with us,
but my Mother, she loves Dartmoor,
and would miss the moor too much.

My Childhood Garden

I will miss this place.
at only the beginning of May
the sun and the garden are shining.
The colours are really brightening up now,
bright enthusiastic yellows,
vigorous reds,
luscious purples.

It's so quiet here.
Only the sounds of the breeze through the trees,
and the birds singing in those trees.
The clicking, tapping noise of Kya as she rolls over and over in
the gravel path is quite pleasing.

And whilst admiring the innocence of this wonder,
I laugh to myself.
Remembering perhaps how it is not so innocent,
(the old wooden table, now supporting various plant pots
smiles at me as it reminisces one other sunny morning).

So many of my summers were spent here in this garden,
and summer parties too!
Is the wolf with red eyes still hiding in the conifer?
I guess I will never know.

We have been here so long that six motors have been here.
(and left here).
Though one still remains to haunt me.
Even two husbands have loved here and left here.

My memories will never leave this garden,
and all my secrets will stay here forever.
Even when we all are gone, the trees will still remember.

Pixies of Devon

A colony of pixie folk are said to live upon the rocks,
they sing and dance all day long, playing havoc quite non-stop.
Near Challacombe upon the moor they meet,
Devonshire pixies with their playful feet.

Near Tavistock on Pixie's Hill, a little cottage lay,
the pixies made it 'home', among tulips every day.
A dear old lady nurtured her garden with pride,
hearing the pixies sing to soothe their babies' cries.

When the sad day came and up to heaven she was shown,
the pixies would appear on the old lady's gravestone.
With her flowers now destroyed, and the pixies forlorn,
on her grave they left tulips, on a little neat lawn.

The pixies though mischievous, are kind and simple folk,
find them on the high moor, or in the woods next to the oak.
They're willing to do good for rewards that are quite small,
the cheeky Devonshire pixies - they look out for one and all!

Dartmoor

From stillness, sweeps in weather not so adorning,
quickly and forceful without prior warning.
A formidable shadow falls west to east,
drowning in darkness, this grey granite beast.

Howling wind slices through the chilled air,
with wickedness waiting to pounce here and there.
Imposing Haytor with its outcrops of stone,
where shadows and darkness engulf you alone.

Not far to the west find creepy Hound Tor,
nascent evil near Widecombe-in-the-Moor.
What do you see in the silhouette of the rocks?
(Perhaps the hounds that froze in a time long forgot).

Hundatora (Hound Tor)

Hundatora stands so imperiously,
haunting ancient moorland mysteriously.
Hundatora wild and ragged,
giant stone stacks windswept and haggard.

Famed for its ghosts and eerie graves,
a settlement dating to Neolithic age.
Famine and plague caused desertion here,
the untamed ambience oppressed with fear.

Close by is the grave of poor Kitty Jay,
with fresh flowers left on her shrine every day.
Hundatora where folk won't merrily meet
for fear of bad soil under their feet.

Horrabridge

Spring lambs lolling about by the side of the road,
make us smile and coo, the fresh little darlings!
Little black and white creatures so wobbly and new.
a drive upon the moor in West Devon with you.

Their protective mama always stays close by to them,
with her mud stained, matted and straggly wool,
looking untidy with her tail long and unkempt.
a peaceful hour upon the moor with you is spent.

See the little wagtails, scuttling along the ground,
black and white just like the gentle lambs we saw,
you know the birds much better than I,
upon the moor where darkness now fills the sky.

You talk of a time some years long gone, when
a sounder of hogs were set free from a farm,
and then came to roam the West Devon moor,
digging up the earth those gluttonous boar!

Breathe in this panoramic vista of Dartmoor,
every tor silhouetted against a moody sky,
splendid views when sun drenches this forbidding landscape,
on the West Devon moor I contemplate life's cruel fate.

Dartmoor Ponies

Dartmoor ponies of Yelverton are
tame and curious, showing no fear.
These Dartmoor ponies are wild and free,
bowing gracefully as they trot near.

Friendly Dartmoor ponies by the aerodrome,
surrounding our car so placid and kind,
kissing the glass with a wet sloppy nose,
inquisitive as to what they may find.

These tough little Dartmoor ponies
are hardy on the harsh open land,
for hundreds of years it's been their home,
untouched by human hand.

Dartmoor ponies near to Yelverton are
gentle and sweet little equine souls.
Dutiful creatures of the moorland,
forever walking their Dartmoor patrol.

Sir Francis Drake

Sir Francis Drake, born in Tavi,
spent his last fifteen years at Buckland Abbey.
Queen Elizabeth found him quite savvy,
when knighted, she thought his gifts rather flashy!

He sailed the globe in The Golden Hind,
many a foreign ship he would find,
he'd capture their cargo (of the gold and silver kind),
leaving the crew a long way behind.
Elizabeth the first, would really admire it,
he was after all her very own pirate!

In fifteen eighty eight, off the Cornish coast,
the people caught sight of the Armada approach,
beacons were lit to deliver the message,
that things were about to get very aggressive!
Drake playing bowls on Plymouth Hoe,
said "there's still time to finish the game before we go!",
(that's likely just a rumour but adds some good humour!).

With the Spaniards defeated - Sir Francis a hero,
he now had his eyes on a ship near Puerto Rico.
With two million ducats and more on board,
he thought to himself, 'I quite fancy that hoard!'.

Sadly for Drake, the voyage did not go to plan,
after no luck with the fighting he became a sick man,
in twenty four hours poor Francis was dead,
and buried in the ocean in a coffin of lead.

Dinner Guests

I love my home on Dartmoor, no other place I'd be,
though I'm amazed at the crazy things I often come to see!
Yesterday, a flock of sheep - a bunch of escapees,
thought they'd pay a visit to my garden for their tea!

Nine sheepish sheep have eaten up my kale,
and all across the lawn they have left a mucky trail.
My spinach and kalettes chewed up by these unruly guests,
they all looked pretty guilty - yet I was not the least impressed.

The other week it was a pair of cheeky feathered thieves,
who had a cunning plan tucked up their feathered sleeves.
When I caught them pecking at the birdies' feed
I asked them politely to "Ruffle up" and leave!

Yet that was seven long winter days ago,
and they didn't comply, I'll have you know!
They're still proudly parading up and down my land
(but they now eat the bird seed right out of my hand!).

Dartmoor Beast!

Menageries of the travelling kind,
19th century or further behind,
escaped, survived then to breed,
on Dartmoor ponies come to feed.

Or beasts released upon the act,
(not lawful now to keep wild cats),
now leave their prints on soft ground,
too wide and strong for any hound.

And farmers mutter of feral cats,
who make the moors their habitat,
savage fiends hunt while we sleep,
and strip the bones of lonely sheep.

Throats slashed by violent claws,
by the wild cats that roam the moors.
The terrible growling heard at night,
terrified yelping as they take a bite.

Sticky blood drips down their teeth,
when on flesh they start to feast,
ripping meat and lapping juices,
livestock steadily reduces.

Then one summers night so mild,
like a puma slinky low and wild,
clearly passed my line of sight,
I saw the beast that very night.

Wembury

Not far away from Plymouth Sound,
a beach with delights to discover,
in Devon, the district of the South Hams,
pretty all year, not only in summer.

Buckets ready to scoop up little creatures,
crabs, shrimps and if you're lucky a shanny!
Oh what fun we had in the rock pools
on Wembury beach last year with granny!

A little stream runs to the ocean,
shallow and warm so splash without care.
(Though don't forget your beach shoes,
the stones may hurt if your feet are bare!).

Sand not so golden like other bays,
a little coarser with shingle of grey,
yet off the beaten track, a beach to roam,
with the iconic landmark, the Great Mewstone.

Bring your binoculars and take a good look,
from the cliff on the South West Coast path.
Will you spot cormorants, a shag, or a rook?
or catch a seal having an afternoon bask!

Running to the shore line, chasing the waves,
my children are thrilled; a great day is spent.
Granny takes us to such wonderful places,
I love to see the joy on my little boys' faces!

Barbican with Dad

Vibrant Barbican days spent with my Dad,
boats bobbing cheerfully, such happy days we had.
We always enjoyed a peaceful meander around,
and the far reaching views out to Plymouth Sound.

You admiring the artwork, for me little gift shops entice,
little boats, or sand in bottles and the art galleries rife!
A pasty from the bakery would make tasty seaside food,
you would buy me ice cream and perhaps some sweeties too.

I still love the barbican, and take my boys to stroll
through the busy streets to see that prawn upon its pole!
Then up to Plymouth Hoe - Smeaton's tower rising tall,
looking down at the seafront and the open air sea pool.

Tavistock with Dad

We often meet for an afternoon in Tavistock,
normally just about 1 o'clock.
You greet us with a smile - always happy,
in excellent spirits - each time joyful and chatty.

We wander at ease to the bakery to eat,
the four of us are shown our seat.
"Three pasties please", the waitress writes with her pen.
"And two sausage rolls, with two gingerbread men!".

We feed the ducks along the canal by meadowlands,
holding tight onto the children's hands,
Ollie was fraught when the ducks swarmed around,
squabbling for the seed with their 'quacking' sound.

A walk by the riverside, the Tavy gushing fast,
nostalgia creeping in as I remember my past,
my school days at Tavi College and the hard times I had,
yet I'll always remember Tavi for the good times with dad.

Jays Grave

In Manaton on Dartmoor,
not far from the infamous Hound Tor,
you'll find the grave of poor Kitty Jay,
quite a phenomena, and quite unexplained
as to why fresh flowers appear every day.

Her bones were dug up
in the late 18th Century,
So we can be sure that there's human remains.
(They were put in a box and buried again).

But who was this woman?
We don't know for sure,
but she lies here alone
with trinkets left upon her headstone.
A curious place of pilgrimage galore,
unsheltered and lonely high up on the moor.

Burrator

There's a sweet smell on the road at the top,
I've never quite worked out what it is,
but I've smelled it there since I was young,
and it's there every time I go back.

Through the narrow stone gate
suddenly open space appears.
An old oak tree I used to climb,
I think back on all those years.

I cry, and sob, and cry again,
I want them back, the years aren't kind.
This place is my true home,
I'm absorbing it all, here on my own.

I'm breathing it in - the granite stone,
the rusty remains of the railway.
The track long gone, I walk along,
Sheepstor reminds me of another day.

Sheep and ponies freely ramble,
this simple life for them is ample,
ragged half sheared and looking tatty,
black and white with wool all matty.

Through the trees a glimpse of the blue,
the man made reservoir now in view,
framed by a skyline of rolling heath,
hear bells from the sunken village beneath.

There's a sweet smell on the road at the top,
I've never quite worked out what it is,
but I've smelled it there since I was young,
and it's there every time I go back.

**NB Though the sunken village myth of Burrator Reservoir
has been disproved, it is still a nice legend to imagine!**

Plymouth

Those cobbled streets so narrow and pretty,
a charming piece of Plymouth City.
the Barbican glistening in the bright sun,
with cheerful people having so much fun.

Colourful and vibrant once standing tall,
a wonderful art work; a splendour for all.
The Lenkiewicz mural was once so bright,
at 3000 square feet it was a marvelous sight.

Dad was acquainted with Lenkiewicz back then,
and commissioned an artwork for him to pen.
He used to pop into the studio whilst waiting,
checking the progress of that perfect painting.

"The house that Jack built" is a curious place,
quite an unusual shopping arcade,
an enchanting forest you'll find inside,
a magical feast for the children's eyes!

Sir Francis Drake still stands at Plymouth Hoe,
where he was when the Armada approached.
By the iconic landmark of Smeaton's Tower,
and the steps where pilgrims set sail the Mayflower.

I remember as a teenager catching the bus
to Plymouth with friends to shop and have lunch.
We'd have a little rest and sit on the sun dial,
and I'd visit my dad at work once in a while.

He was once the head chef at the Holiday Inn,
the tall hotel on Plymouth Hoe, where within
for royals, politicians and the famous he prepared
delicious meals showing how much he cared.

Brean Down (Somerset)

Daring goats cling without fear on the sheer cliff edge,
at Brean Down in Somerset the flat sand bay stretches west.

Endless steps up to the top of Brean Down, the wind strong.
a greeting cold on our cheeks - a fierce chill we meet.

Fresh air blows the cobwebs off, with sea either side,
wild and gusty along the thin peninsula we stride.

Not at all poor for an hour's drive from the city,
a stone's throw to the country and in its own way quite pretty.

Though murky sea does not shine so gloriously,
but one can't complain of this tempestuous terrain.

Then all battered at the very end of the course,
desolate remains of a fort, face the wind's force.

Wookey Hole

Stalagmites and stalactites.
walk through the cave - dark as night,
unsteady and rough beneath our feet,
as we lose the warmth of outside heat.

Fifty thousand years in the past,
early men occupied these caverns vast.
Hunting rhinoceros and bear was a knack,
you had to learn quick if you wanted a snack!

But deep in the chambers down below
lived a woman, her dog and a couple of goats,
she was thought a witch - evil and immoral,
and blamed on wrong doing and causing sorrow.

The villagers frightfully up in arms
wanted to kill the witch and her sinful charms.
To ensure evil magic could not survive,
Father Bernard was called to exorcise.

So from neighbouring Glastonbury Abbey,
came Father Bernard to end the witch so scraggy,
with a candle and bible as his weapon of favour,
stooping over her cooking pot he looked right at her!

He tried to talk but she screamed out a curse,
she fled deep into the cavern still crying her verse!
Father Bernard scooped water from the river on stone,
blessed it by Christ and threw it at the old crone.

The Witch of Wookey convulsively stiffened,
(who knows, if she had have listened),
but now we see her poor figure solidified,
a legacy of the hag in the cave where she died.

Clevedon

Spending time today with you son,
has been such a delight.
Just you and I, with no little brother for you to fight.
In Clevedon we had fun catching crabs,
we caught so many!
(In Looe we hardly caught any).
Well done my little energetic boy,
you were so sweet without your little brother to annoy!

Westonbirt Arboretum

A stroll through the arboretum,
among the tallest trees,
summer's long gone,
feel the autumn breeze.
So tranquil in the woods,
where no city sounds you'll hear,
though little animals hide and scurry
secretly always near!

Acton Court

500 years ago, a mere handshake away,
Henry VIII and his queen had a visit to pay,
they spent two nights at Acton Court,
during their mission to gain more support.

Nearly black elm-wood under my feet,
the exact same flooring where kings soles once did meet.
What have the walls in this chamber absorbed?
They must hold the secrets and whispers once forged.

Extravagant beauty King Henry admired
and his tapestries hung here just how he desired.
To imagine deeply what happened in this home,
sends shivers tingling through my bones!

Oh Anne Boleyn, Anne Boleyn,
if only you knew the future, where in,
just nine months later you'd be labelled a traitor,
and on the 19th of May at 8 o'clock,
you'd lay your head down on the block…

Now rescued from a sorry state of disrepair,
no longer so shabby with no one to care.
Acton Court is restored to its righteous glory,
and is awaiting to tell you the rest of its story.

A Hardy Adventure

At Hardy's birth place we explore,
ducking our heads under every door,
a wild garden with flowers in bloom,
for a family of six there wasn't much room!

Then to Max Gate, with décor quite like,
the taste of my mother's - such a delight!
Maroon coloured walls with fireplace grey,
great minds think alike (isn't that what they say?).

Continuing our journey onto Clouds Hill,
where the topsy turvy cottage looks lived in still,
T.E Lawrence returned from a desert at war,
tragic to think of what fate had in store.

An oyster shell bay, just us girls together,
a perfect close to our "Hardy" adventure,
studying with interest the rock formation,
Lulworth Cove – a geology education!

Before the drive home with the turn of the key,
we devour fish and chips and mushy peas.
Satisfied from a day of "novel" escape,
we must hit the road as it's really quite late!

Country Life Vs City Life

City life, city strife,
strap yourself in and hold on tight!
Faster faster! Can't lose pace!
(You have got to win this race)

Country life, rolling tide,
Dartmoor mystery, natural history,
slowly, slowly, rest is rife,
relax… Enjoy the countryside…

Lancaut Nature Reserve

The fog was low and the air was mild,
misty mud banks gave a sense of the wild,
so forget we're in Wales, just for a while,
enjoying the trek for three little miles.

Leaf covered tracks, passing cliffs so tall,
climbing nimbly over a giant rock fall,
carefully stepping, being sure not to fall,
out to the glade feeling so mystical.

Next ascending to the high reaching precipice,
dizzying heights with the path wet and treacherous,
this stroll cleared my mind, and was truly adventurous,
just nature, the woodland and the chatter between us.

The Goblin

Grotesque and ill-mannered a creature
(with not one defining beauty feature).
He shuffles 'round planning no good deed -
a small selfish being with a heart full of greed.

Smashing pots and pans in the dead of night,
dropping dishes to give you a fright.
The Goblin is up to no good at all,
he'll snatch your quilt - even though he is small.

Malicious and sly – you should watch your step,
he is quite an ugly and miserable wretch,
and if you should hear a loud crashing sound
it would be him dragging the furniture 'round!

Gold and silver he heartily desires,
smuggling it back to his cavern of fire.
Dark and dismal in his covert abode,
troublesome to humans and vengeful I'm told.

Goblin, Goblin don't come near,
stay away - stop spreading fear.
Short in stature with stubby toes,
return to your hole where nothing grows!

Sirens of the Sea

Half bird, half wanton women,
singing songs of pure temptation.
Sweet voice emanating from the rocks,
feathered temptress spread your wings -
lure sailors in as your lost soul sings.

The compass knows not east nor west,
in distress she drags wandering men
to seek comfort within her wicked wings.
Yet some know the dangers creatures cast,
so tie themselves onto their masts.

Circe gave warnings of these sirens
to Odysseus on his journey from war,
"pass these Sirens by, steer clear from their lair -
beware their deceptive sweetened grace,
do not be fooled by their pretty face".

Heading God's words with wax in their ears,
for fear of being caught in their trap.
Music playing with bewitching clarity,
some ill-fated seafarers never reach home,
but lie rotting in a meadow of flesh and bone.

For the only joy these Sirens will feed on
is destroying life of luckless prey,
with feet as a bird and face of a woman,
an enchantress of the ocean wide,
so be on your guard, sailors passing by!

Selkie

I gaze lusting out to sea
from my window longing endlessly,
to my home among the scaled and finned,
for my mortal husband has stolen my skin.

Trapped on land there is some comfort
yet even so I am distraught.
Remembering when I came to shore,
peeled off my suit then swam no more.

I bore two children - both so sweet,
they know not their grandma without feet.
She bobs her head up from the foam,
and prays I will return to home.

I wonder if my sweet offspring
will discover such a wondrous thing,
and without intention bring to me,
my skin to send me back to sea.

Hampton Court Palace

We start at Base Court, a fine and impressive entry,
imagine courtiers bustling back and forth in the 16th century.
The awe hits me fiercely like a deep rooted intimacy,
this palace of red brick is a rich place of history.

Henry VIII's kitchens enormous and beyond belief,
roasting up wild boar, deer, oxen and beef.
The cooks sweltering with exhaustion; working tirelessly,
to feed the four hundred mouths of the palace's entirety.

Standing in the Great Hall at Hampton Court Palace,
breathing in energy five centuries long since passed.
Presence of Anne Boleyn and each ill-fated queen,
echoing wall to wall where celebrations were once seen.

Tapestries then shimmering and sparkling with gold,
absorbed all the whispering and stories once told,
I close my eyes to come close to the spirits and ghosts,
where once king and queens liked to dance the most.

Through the Great Watching Chamber to the gallery, where
Catherine escaped her guards and ran to reach Henry at prayer,
to the Chapel Royal she screamed for mercy in attempt to spare
her young sweet life - to no avail, for the King had no care.

The Royal Pew - stand where he would have once prayed,
the view of the chapel where Jane Seymour's heart stayed,
with its intricate ceiling of blue and gold will amaze,
a church where for centuries Monarchs have praised.

Hampton Court Palace is a mix of bygone times,
yet my affection always wanders to the first two wives
and the gruesome way Anne and the fifth lost their lives.
She wept, "Good Christian people, I have come here to die".

Catherine of Aragon

A Princess leaving my Spanish realm,
I Catherine, with my captain at the helm,
longing to see mamá y papá again,
fearing of life, no longer the same.

Betrothed since the age of three,
I sailed across the ocean to thee,
to Arthur, my English Prince and heir,
to the throne, of which I soon would share.

I was just sixteen years of age,
sailing into a life pre-arranged,
not imagining how fate would rule
(my reign to end in a way so cruel).

We were married in fifteen hundred and one,
tragically our marriage had but begun,
when we were parted from one another,
and then I was to marry Henry, your brother.

How cruel and unforgiving life was to me,
I, true Queen of England so withdrawn,
how could I forgive him for what *he* did?
(My crime was that no son did live).

Mary sweet Mary, child of mine,
no longer in the Monarch's line.
He, the King, denied me her touch,
I missed my sweet Mary, so very much.

I'm dying now - life has almost left,
fifty years and now with poisoned flesh.
My faithful maid flocks to my side,
and in my last days to him I write –

"My most dear lord, husband and king,
I pardon you for everything.
I pray that God will pardon you too,
please give to my maids what they are due,

I commend unto you, Mary our daughter,
beseeching you to be a good father,
mine eyes desire you above all things,
from your only true wife,
Catherine the Queen".

Tessy Braun

Anne Boleyn

You were my good Lord
and handsome you once were,
though your affection over me
had caused quite some stir.
For England adored Catherine,
who was your Queen before,
and they had the *audacity* to call me
a "Goggle eyed whore!".

Your love first fell on my sister
in the French Court,
but your lust for her,
like many girls
was really rather short.
My seductive dark brown eyes
captured your kindly attention,
yet to become a mere mistress,
was never my chosen intention.

It wasn't long before you understood
it was *"Queen or nothing"*,
with your dreams of son and heir,
this only inspired your lusting.
Wolsey got to work
with the Pope to arrange the divorce,
he gave you false hope that it would be
just a matter of course.

You clung to the view
marriage to *her* was against God's Law,
for she had lain in bed
with your dear brother before.
Yet Pope Clement VII
would not fight our cause,
so you broke from the Catholic Church
and its ridiculous rules.

For me! My goodly Lord,
for me you changed the Christian faith!
(How could anyone have known
I'd soon be fallen from your grace?)
but then, instead of a goodly prince,
I bore you a female child,
and with the loss of others,
it seems God would have you riled.

I was never very popular
and many thought me cursed,
rumours spread I had six fingers,
warts and that is not the worst.
I couldn't give the King a son,
so my cruel demise began,
they made it up - I didn't lie with my brother,
or take another man.

Fallen from your favour
and your attention now on Jane,
my father's greedy ambition
had put us all in shame.
They made it all up,
Smeaton my dear friend,
they tortured him until
he said what they *wanted* to hear.
(Yet he met his death on Tower Hill).

My goodly lord I spent nights and days
preparing for my leave of this world,
My brother gone, my heart did grieve.

It's agonisingly postponed
for the swordsman's arrival, yet
he travels so kindly from France
to slice through my little neck.

"And thus I take my leave
of the world and of you all,
oh Lord have mercy on me,

to God I commend my soul".
and with my ladies sobbing
silently by my side,
my head falls to the ground
but my soul is still alive!

Jane Seymour

Loved was I, cherished quite,
for I brought him a steady light,
I was not wicked, fierce or strong,
in his kingly eyes I did no wrong.

As Anne's lady in waiting, I could see
the King's attention fall on me,
just a day after she lost her head
the king promised to wed me instead.

We married yet I was never crowned,
for that pesky plague was still around.
I was kind and compassionate to Mary,
All of court thought me pleasant and caring.

Soon I was with child - my belly swelled,
not foreseeing the sorrow, the future held.
After a labour of two nights and three days,
I was fiercely struck with agonising pain.

I died! Leaving my son with no mother.
He mourned, he could not love another.
Yet there was good news
throughout the court,
for the King had the son
he had long sought!

He always *thought* I was his favourite wife,
but I wonder if I hadn't lost my life,
perhaps he would have tired soon after,
it's likely my life would have been a disaster.
Now we lie together once more,
at Windsor Castle in
'The Chapel of St George'.
Edward ruled at the tender age of nine,
but tuberculosis took him,
poor child of mine.

Anne Of Cleves

I was the plain German Princess,
Holbein came to paint my face,
so that my presence Henry could witness,
a fine portrait for his grace.

Cromwell did quite insist
that a match was made with us.
In the wake of the "Truce of Nice"
it would not be a marriage unjust.

One might say that I was the lucky one,
for I came out of it all unscathed,
for Henry did not find me pretty,
I was not the woman he craved.

He said I was ugly and *most* unclean,
yet he was the one with the odour.
His ulcer repulsively obscene,
and he thought me mediocre!?

When an annulment he asked of me,
I'd have been a fool to object,
so I agreed to it wholeheartedly,
this would *surely* save my neck?

The "King's dear sister" I was known,
he gave me Richmond Palace and more.
I was quite happy to give up the throne,
his generosity could not be ignored.

I, the only wife in Westminster Abbey,
some have found my tomb hard to find,
I was aged only forty-one when I passed,
and I was the last of his wives to die.

Tessy Braun

Catherine Howard

I was but a child, not grown in years or mind.
life was cut short
and I left this cruel world behind.

On the 13th February
on death's path I tread,
when Henry VIII cuts off my sweet head!

My demise, though tragic,
was not foreseen,
despite the fate of the last fallen queen,
my first cousin Anne Boleyn…

*(I had briefly forgot,
that she had laid her head upon the block!).*

Yet fancy of court and royal life
was too appetizing,
with my flirtatious and fun loving nature,
was it surprising
that the ever growing wider Henry VIII
became so besotted
with my pretty young face?

I was his rose without a thorn,
but I found him disgusting.
His hideous ulcer repulsed me
and with his gut busting,
is it any wonder I looked about the Court
for something better,
of course I had my eyes set
on Thomas Culpeper!

I was immature, and raised
in a house of permissiveness.
My greatest crime
was my emotional silliness.

They came to take me
"give me mercy" I screamed,
for some hope still remained
that I might be redeemed.

Yet down the river I went
to the Tower by water,
passing under London Bridge
I am reminded of the slaughter
that awaits me.
I am asked to prepare my soul for death,
I ask for the block,
to see how I will place myself best.

I could barely speak, yet confessed
my wrong doing in a weak voice.
I knelt, and with one quick swing of the axe my meek life was
gone,
my body covered with a cloak
and taken away
by my ladies,
to the Chapel of St Peter in chains.

Catherine Parr

Last, but by no means least,
I wed Henry VIII, hideous and obese,
at Hampton Court Palace,
we made our vows
to be man and wife as law allows.

It was fifteen forty-three,
you had grown quite smitten with me,
you were a king
who could not be refused,
so this was the life that I *had* to choose.

With plague around the London streets,
for six months we stayed away
in our palace retreat,
in company together we built a foundation,
and we got along well, without hesitation.

It helped that we had interests shared
of music, archery and hunting we both cared,
when you fought in France
for the very last time,
you left me to reign
as if the throne were mine.

I loved Mary and Elizabeth as my own,
and watched over them
until they were grown,
restoring your daughters
to the succession line,
and I cared for Edward
(but that poor lamb died).

Some say I couldn't have possibly
loved you truly, dear,
being a tyrant and filling your
kingdom with fear,

but I accepted this life as God's true will,
(and made quite sure
you had *no* reason to kill),

but when you took a last breath
into your lungs
I was relieved for my life had just begun,
now free to re-marry,
with riches, I could rejoice,
and Thomas Seymour was my choice!

So now with my true love
I was reconciled,
A miracle happened
when I became with child,
but with my wildest dreams,
came my death curse,
I left my sweet daughter
eight days after her birth.

I was laid to rest at St Mary's Chapel,
in my beautiful home at Sudeley Castle,
but after more than two hundred years,
my coffin was found
and my flesh re-appeared.

Wrapped up snuggly in cloth,
resting in peace,
disturbed from my slumber,
ripped open my sheets,
the flesh on my arm
was still moist and white,
and when they unearthed
me I gave them a fright!

After my embalmed wax linen
was cut and frayed,
my skin turned brown
and my flesh decayed,
but taken from me was a lock of hair,
and a tooth of mine for all to share.

Tessy Braun

Porthcurno, Cornwall

The sea is always such a wonderful turquoise colour at Porthcurno,
and when paired with the dazzling near white sand, one could
imagine being in the Mediterranean or even the Caribbean! The
image on the front cover of this book is a painting created by myself
based on this photograph. This picture was taken on a beautiful day
in October, and the only clue that it isn't the height of summer is the
fact that the beach isn't overcrowded, and there's nobody in the sea!
The incredible Minack Theatre clings to the cliff just west of
Porthcurno beach, and is very much worth a visit.

(Read my poem about Porthcurno on pg. 7 & 8)

Photograph taken by Tessy Braun

St Ives, Cornwall

Here is a beautiful photograph showcasing the wonderful mixture of colours in St Ives. Just look at those pretty boats bobbing around in the water! Many days have been spent enjoying the little town beach with my boys, and taking pleasure in this idyllic seaside town. There's usually a grey seal or two in the harbour waiting to say hello, and you'll see even more seals if you take a trip out to "Seal Island" (also known as The Carracks). St Ives is one of my favourite locations in Cornwall, and it is a favourite place for artists all around the world due to its wonderful elevated light levels.

(Read my poem about St Ives on pg. 4)

Photograph taken by Michael Elliott

Minack Theatre, Cornwall

The Minack must be the most unique and spectacular theatre in the world with its dramatic views across the Atlantic. We have paid a visit during the day time on many occasions over the years, yet have never actually been to see a performance there. I would like to see a show at The Minack Theatre at some point in the future. As part of the day visit we saw a story teller tell tales of Cornish myths which was an enchanting experience. To the east of the theatre, which is carved into the cliff, you'll find Porthcurno beach. There is a cliff path that can be taken down to the beach; however it is definitely not for the faint hearted – I much prefer to use the car park for a less hair raising journey down to this spectacular bay!

(Read my poem about the Minack Theatre on pg. 9).

Photograph taken by Tessy Braun

St Michael's Mount, Cornwall

St Michael's Mount - a location submerged in myth and legend. This photograph was taken by my son's father when he was taking a cycle tour of West Cornwall. This tidal island holds many interesting things to explore with its rich history and folklore. It's a lot of fun walking to the island on the cobble stone causeway which is exposed between mid-tide and low water.   Can you imagine Cormoran the Giant reaching out and plucking children or cattle from the mainland?

(Read my poem about St Michael's Mount on pg. 12)

Photograph taken by Michael Elliott

Land's End, Cornwall

Rugged and dramatic landscape at Land's End in this picture taken in October 2016. I love to walk along the coastal path at Land's End and take in the breath-taking views across the Atlantic Ocean. (There are some amazing spots to perch on to enjoy them). It's more than often very windy here as you face the open sea. As well as the glorious scenery at Land's End you'll also find lots of other things to do so and see with children, including a King Arthur's Quest exhibit, a 4D cinema, a 200 year old farm and many other attractions. However for me, the main appeal is the magnificent coastal setting and the feeling of freedom one gets from being there.

(Read my poem about Land's End on pg. 16).

Photograph taken by Tessy Braun

Chûn Quoit, Cornwall

When I take my boys on holiday we tend to go out on expeditions in
the countryside. Often in Cornwall we set off looking for ancient
standing stones and stone circles. In this photo you see the
impressive Chûn Quoit in West Cornwall on the open moor. When
we found this Neolithic Tomb it was quite a last minute detour. On
this occasion we were driving along the wonderful North Cornwall
coastal road from St Ives to Land's End when we decided to come
off the road and attempt to locate Chûn Quoit. We parked by a
remote farm house, not knowing for certain that it was the correct
starting place. However luck was on our side that day and as we
hiked up the hill we found Chûn Castle on our right, and soon in our
line of sight was the impressive monument that you see in the photo.

(Read my poem about Cornish standing stones on pg. 13)

Photograph taken by Tessy Braun

Black Head, St Austell, Cornwall

I remember this day fondly. My mother and I, along with my two boys went to find the A.L Rowse monument up on Black Head. My mother inspired an interest within me in regards to the late Cornish historian and poet after sharing some of his work with me. It was a stifling hot day and we all have very warm memories from the lovely walk. We strolled past cows in the adjacent fields, and my children were not too keen on the very close proximity to them! The hedges were full of blackberries which we enjoyed picking. The memorial was easily found and we enjoyed a cup of tea from our flask when we reached it. If you are not familiar with A.L Rowse I recommend that you read about his life and poetry. One of my favourite poems Rowse wrote is called "Gear" where he describes the sometimes peculiar nature of Cornwall.

(Read my poem about Black Head on pg. 21).

Photograph taken by Tessy Braun

Widemouth Bay, Cornwall

A favourite place to go when staying at my mum's house in West
Devon. Widemouth Bay, near Bude is a great place to go body
boarding. It is a very convenient beach to visit because the car park is
directly by the beach which means there is no need to carry beach
equipment very far. As you can see in the photograph there is a
border of giant rocks which my children tend to enjoy climbing on.
The beach is a mixture of sand and pebbles. We've found some
beautiful stones in the past with lovely white markings. In addition
to the beach to enjoy, there is a wonderful cliff walk to the east, with
glorious views. On one occasion we were fortunate enough to see
the Cornwall Air Ambulance, and my boys were invited inside – it
goes without saying that they were delighted with this opportunity!

(Read my poem about Widemouth Bay on pg. 19).

Photograph taken by Tessy Braun

Burrator Reservoir, West Devon

I grew up in a small village on the edge of Dartmoor, close to the
beautiful Burrator Reservoir. My boys and I love to walk over the
moors to Sheepstor, which you can see in the background of this
photograph. We once had a wonderful adventure climbing to the top!
Along this route lie still the remains of the Burrator and Sheepstor
Halt railway, which once ran from Yelverton to Princetown. Burrator
is a very peaceful place to live and I miss it very much now that I am
an adult. I often wish that I did not move away to the city all those
years ago. One day I would like to live in the countryside again, but
for now my life is in Bristol, and we are very lucky here that there are
many lovely green spaces in the city and nearby.

(Read my poems about Burrator on pg. 35 and pg. 50)

Photograph taken by Tessy Braun

Brean Down, Somerset

After a relatively short drive from Bristol I am able to reach the countryside and escape from the city for a short time. When one is used to the blue seas of Cornwall and Devon, the murky waters of the Bristol Channel can seem a little drab, but nevertheless Brean Down is a lovely refreshing place to walk and clear your mind. At the end of the peninsula lie the remains of a ruined fort that was used in World War II, though has a history of people dwelling there as far back as the Stone Age.

(Read my poem about Brean Down on pg. 52)

Photograph taken by Tessy Braun

My Boys at St Ives Bay Holiday Park

This holiday park is my all-time favourite place to go in Cornwall. We've been going there as a family since I was a small child and it holds a myriad of special memories for me. I now bring my own two boys to this beautiful holiday park every year, and not always in the summer, October can be a great time to visit! They love exploring the "Upton Towans", a large stretch of sand dunes which hold the remains of an old dynamite factory. The beach is several miles long, and the Godrevy Lighthouse is a famous landmark of the area. I have written a poem about this lovely holiday park which you can find on pg. 2 of this book.

Photograph taken by Tessy Braun

A picture of me and my sister with our parents

(Left to right: Rosemary Braun, Gabi Stedman-Braun, Tessy Braun, Gerhard Braun).

Family times are not always perfect, but my family are perfect to me and so very important. My family have always been there for me when I am in need, and I appreciate and love them so much. I urge you to never take your family for granted, because you never know what may be around the corner and how quickly things may change one way or another. A special mention to my sister Gabi, who really has helped me so much over the years, and of course to my two beautiful little boys, Oliver and Joshua xx

Photograph taken by Oliver Braun, May 2018

ABOUT THE AUTHOR

Tessy has been writing poems and short stories since she was a child. Tucked away in her home you'll find boxes of diaries and journals that are testimony to her love of writing.

Having grown up in a remote village on the edge of Dartmoor, with many family holidays spent in Cornwall, Tessy found plenty of inspiration for the poems she has written.

Having recently shared samples of her writing on Instagram, (**@poems_by_tessy**), Tessy was inspired to finally get her words in print.

Other titles include:

For None Would Hear
A poetic story exploring the tragic consequences of domestic abuse

Open Book
A collection of poetry exploring a range of themes including love, heartbreak, abuse, depression, parenting and loss.

In addition to writing, Tessy is also a keen musician and enjoys playing the cello and violin. Tessy is also mother of two young boys and enjoys sharing her local knowledge when taking her children to beautiful places in the West Country and beyond!

Printed in Poland
by Amazon Fulfillment
Poland Sp. z o.o., Wrocław

53364260R00061